THE CONGRESSIONAL HANDBOOK

Simple Lessons on Healing Our Broken Government

D. M. RIACH

The contents of this work, including, but not limited to, the accuracy of events, people, and places depicted; opinions expressed; permission to use previously published materials included; and any advice given or actions advocated are solely the responsibility of the author, who assumes all liability for said work and indemnifies the publisher against any claims stemming from publication of the work.

All Rights Reserved
Copyright © 2022 by D. M. Riach

No part of this book may be reproduced or transmitted, downloaded, distributed, reverse engineered, or stored in or introduced into any information storage and retrieval system, in any form or by any means, including photocopying and recording, whether electronic or mechanical, now known or hereinafter invented without permission in writing from the publisher.

Dorrance Publishing Co
585 Alpha Drive
Suite 103
Pittsburgh, PA 15238
Visit our website at www.dorrancebookstore.com

ISBN: 979-8-8860-4209-2
eISBN: 979-8-8860-4862-9

INTRODUCTION

Here we are at the beginning of 2022, having survived five or six years of the most incredible political theater since Caesar called out Brutus. Four years of leadership under one of the most unique individuals ever to hold the office of President of the United States of America. You loved him or you despised him, no middle ground. Long after the current crop of so-called journalists, entertainers and other ne'er-do-wells have passed away, long after the self-anointed intellectual elites have been forgotten, history will decide the value of that presidency.

Then came the pandemic, a word most people had never heard of before. A whole new list of "experts" appeared overnight, the media and the chattering class hanging on to their every word, desperately looking for some clarity and leadership.

Our elected representatives, the ones that profess great leadership skills when things are going well, were more than happy to turn this hot potato over to a largely unknown group of bureaucrats who had been buried for decades in various federal and state government bureaucracies. Many of these newfound experts relished in the spotlight, granting interviews, commenting on anything and everything to a totally confused and misinformed press and general public.

But the most damaging human trait, the lust for power, emerged when our representatives cowered in confusion and permitted governors and mayors virtually unlimited emergency powers to control our daily lives. Many of those scoundrels did just that, brandishing their newfound power through edicts demanding the wearing of face masks, imposing social distancing rules and selectively shutting down businesses in their states. It will take years to undo the damage done by the most brazen of these jerks.

At the same time, the 2020 election cycle wraps up and voila, a new savior was anointed! We are now one year into that reign with a tidal wave of voter remorse sweeping the country.

Some would look to Congress for leadership. That is probably the ultimate definition of an oxymoron. Our United States Congress, both at the leadership and the general member levels, is a colossal embarrassment to "We, the People."

Why is that? How did we devolve to this dreadful state?

I'm just an average guy, one of the masses living in flyover country, paying my taxes and expecting something reasonable in return. I'm holding up my end of the bargain.

It occurred to me that perhaps many of our elected representatives don't seem to have a clue as to what they are supposed to do and, even worse, don't understand and won't accept any responsibility that goes along with the position they so covet.

It's not just the politicians that demonstrate this responsibility deficit.

While preparing this handbook it became more and more obvious that an even greater danger may be the massive number of ill-informed voters in this country who have also demonstrated a significant responsibility deficit. Do these voters really understand who they are voting for and what choices are being offered to them? Do they truly understand the issues and the policies being presented or are they simply following the crowd?

These questions apply both to the political candidate and to the voter. For politicians, the answer is easier to detect based on their performance or lack thereof in office. The questions are more challenging when it comes to the voter who is shielded by the secret ballot and supposed freedom of individual choice. Some people may well understand they are voting for an idiot, they just like the alternative even less!

We all need a refresher course in basic civics, understanding how our government should work. This handbook outlines several areas where improvements in basic understanding of the political process would significantly benefit the performance of our country.

I hope this becomes a treasured reference manual and provides a framework for moving this great country forward once again.

The Congressional Handbook

☆ ☆ ☆
LESSON PLAN

The U.S. Constitution 1

Election Integrity 5

Voter Responsibility 11

The Pandemic 17

Emergency Powers 21

Expiration Dates 25

Climate Change 29

Accountability 33

Concentration of Power 37

Social Justice 43

Muddled Thinking 49

Immigration Policy 53

Education 59

Epilogue 63

LESSON ONE ☆ ☆ ☆
THE U.S. CONSTITUTION

The original Constitution of the United States of America, created in September of 1787, was only four pages long with a total of 4608 words. The twenty-seven amendments enacted since then only add a few additional pages.

Please read it.

It is not that difficult. Some of terminology used is not consistent with today's English language. If you are having trouble, call a friend. If nothing else, remember and absorb the first three words "We the People."

We the People established the Constitution, which sets out the basic structure for the three co-equal branches of our government—Congress, the Executive Branch and the Judiciary Branch—and outlines the powers and limitations of each branch. The Constitution is a straightforward set of instructions on how our country should work, summarized as follows:

Article I

The Legislative Branch, consisting of the House of Representatives and the Senate, has the sole power to make and pass laws, to borrow money for the nation, to create and fund the military and to check and balance the Executive and Judicial branches.

Article II

The Executive Branch manages the daily operations of the Federal government through the various federal departments and agencies in accordance with the laws passed by Congress. The President, elected nationally for a term of four years through an electoral college process, is head of the Executive Branch, commander-in-chief of the military, conducts foreign policy and updates Congress on the State of the Union. Presidential power is not unlimited.

Article III

Deals with the Supreme Court including issues of lifetime appointments and the breadth of jurisdiction.

Article IV

Defines the relationship between the federal government and the States, including how new States can be added to the Union.

Article V

The processes for revising the Constitution is set out in this article.

Article VI

Affirms the Constitution and all subsequent laws are "the supreme Law of the Land." All government officials, elected representatives or senators, or members of the judicial or executive branches whether state or federal must swear an oath to uphold the Constitution.

Article VII

Outlines the ratification process for establishing the Constitution. It lists names of the people who signed the Constitution as representatives for twelve of the original thirteen states. Rhode Island ratified the Constitution three years later, in May of 1790.

A remarkable document! The Constitution along with its several amendments defines the role of government, its responsibilities and its limitations. Seven articles reaffirming that We the People set the rules, not you the politicians and bureaucrats. It sets out that Congress, the Executive Branch and the Judicial Branch have only the enumerated and limited powers noted therein. Any powers not defined in the Constitution are left to the State(s).

If you and your constituents disagree with any of the terms of the Constitution, Article V sets out precisely how the Constitution can be amended. Make your case, follow the process and get it changed!

If your case is not strong enough to secure an amendment, quit complaining.

This original version is what most people think of when talking about the Constitution. In fact, there are two versions of the Constitution, the original version and the current operating version, which is 2,862 pages long! This long version, often referred to as the "Constitution Annotated," includes the analysis and interpretation of the Supreme Court decisions that have clarified or otherwise affected the original Constitution. This document is published as Senate Document Numbered 39,[1] updated every ten or so years (most recent edition dated June 27, 2016), and is prepared by the Congressional Research Service of the Library of Congress. It is available to the public in either hardbound or online versions.

The legislators all receive free copies. A total of 3,870 hardbound versions are made available to all members of the House and Senate. I wonder how many legislators have read their copy of the Constitution Annotated.

This long form of the Constitution is essentially what we know as the law of the land. Legislators create statutes that become law when enacted. If those statutes were written in a clear and unambiguous manner, they become one more law that we must endure. When those statutes are poorly written or are biased or ambiguous (which has become all too common in recent years), they are likely to be challenged in the courts, often ending up in the Supreme Court. The resulting Supreme Court decisions may or may not be consistent with the original intentions of the elected legislators.

This is not the fault of the Supreme Court. It is a failure of the legislators to do their job in a responsible, professional and timely manner.

As a legislator, you can propose new laws or revise prior laws to satisfy the wishes of your constituents. Do your job. Draft a law or amendment that is specific, clear, concise and unambiguous. Then work with your colleagues on both sides to get it passed through Congress. If Congress doesn't pass it, maybe it wasn't such a good proposition in the first place.

Evading your responsibility by attempting to circumvent the Congressional legislative process through Judiciary rulings (or through Executive Orders) is an unacceptable and somewhat adolescent approach. Do a better job of writing proposed laws in the first place.

What's the lesson here?

This country is a Federal Republic, formed under a Constitution designed to provide a strong federal government with limited authority. As an elected official, the Constitution is the rulebook for your actions. Not party policy, political ideology, media opinion, pressure from lobbyists nor your personal desire for reelection.

"The Constitution is not a document for the government to restrain the people: it is an instrument for the people to restrain the government."
—Patrick Henry

LESSON TWO ☆ ☆ ☆
ELECTION INTEGRITY

Election integrity is all about ensuring every legitimate voter can vote confidentially and without inducement or fear of retribution, that all legitimate voters are granted reasonable access to voting places and that all votes are accurately counted in a timely manner.

The responsibility for conducting elections rests with the individual states, not with the federal government. Each state determines its own rules for voter registration, voter identification, number and location of voting stations, voting hours, early voting procedures (if any), tabulating processes, etc. The result is 50 sets of roughly similar rules with minor differences state to state, but all sharing one overarching principle.

Every citizen is entitled to one vote and one vote only.

Verifying that every vote is a legitimate vote is an essential step in assuring election integrity. It is not voter suppression. Verification processes for in-person voting have been well developed over the years and are generally considered credible. The recent significant increase in the amount of mail-in voting has exposed the much weaker or in some cases nonexistent requirement for mail-in voter identification, seriously eroding public confidence in election integrity.

All votes need to be cast before the end of election day and should be counted without delay or interruption. Counting votes that can't be confirmed as being cast before close of voting hours only sheds doubt on the integrity of the voting process.

The term fraud can be broadly defined[2] as the use of deceit, trickery, or illegal practice to deceive others or to gain some unfair or dishonest advantage.

Remarkably similar to how many people would describe political campaigns!

As long as there have been elections, voter fraud has existed. In varying degrees, sometimes subtle and insignificant, sometimes outrageously obvious yet often unchallenged.

In modern federal election cycles, hundreds of millions and possibly billions of dollars are spent on election campaigns across the nation. Where does that money go?

At the small end, campaign operatives might "get out the vote" by picking up people in neighborhoods and giving them rides to the polling booths. This could also include a coffee or free meal along the way. I lived in the Chicago area for several years where the voting Precinct Captains allegedly referred to funding for this practice as "walking around money."

At the other end of the scale is the outrageous amount of money spent on campaign promotions and advertisements, most often focused on digging up dirt on an opposing candidate. If they couldn't find any dirt, some campaign operatives have allegedly created dirt by using seemingly plausible scenarios to lambaste their competitor (Steele dossier?).

The dirt, real or imagined, is then used in creating some flashy or just plain sickening advertisement and running that ad endlessly on seemingly every TV and radio station, and on countless billboards and in printed media. As election day approaches, this political smog settles over the country, choking out any remaining access to reality.

While some find this entertaining, too many actually believe some of the garbage presented in these ads and vote accordingly!

Where does this money come from? Is it all identified and duly recorded under the rules of the Federal Election Commission[3] (FEC), the organization that we are told can assure us of complete transparency when it comes to seeing who is paying for all these ads?

There have been numerous investigations into allegations of election fraud, usually ending with a report stating there was no evidence of fraud found.

"No evidence of fraud found." What exactly does that statement mean?

It doesn't mean there was no fraud, only that none was discovered. So what can we do about it?

Some would say we need to pass legislation limiting the amount of dollars spent on elections. Don't be naive. Free and fair elections are a largely fictitious concept. The thirst for power is rampant across the political class and the money will follow regardless of mere laws or regulations.[4] The money flow won't ever stop but it can change direction when the votes change. Even dark money won't chase a loser!

There is a term used in the plumbing industry know as bowl siphoning,[5] the natural phenomenon that enables a toilet to flush. If you pour several cups of water into a toilet one cup at a time, nothing happens. The water level in the bowl doesn't change. If you take a bucket full of water and dump it quickly into the toilet, the level rises slightly then whoosh, it all flushes down the drain! Bowl siphoning in action.

Now think about election cycles and the modern-day campaign process. Candidates plead for contributions to their election campaign, proudly noting that whatever amount, large or small will help assure the success of the candidate and the positions supported by that candidate. Bragging rights are awarded to the candidates with large numbers of small donations. This somehow demonstrates to the world that such candidate is held in high esteem by the masses.

Like several cups of water, large numbers of small donations may temporarily benefit the candidate but won't really impact the level or direction of the campaign.

Then along comes the bucket of water in the form of huge slugs of funds from individuals or organizations such as corporations or unions, all looking for special attention from the candidate. Don't forget about the occasional bucketful of dark money that comes from wherever, even from foreign sources.

Whoosh! There goes the impact of the little cup-full-sized donations from the highly esteemed masses!

The good intentions of at least a couple generations of gullible supporters have likely already suffered this fate.

It is up to the voter to counterbalance the impact of all this money flowing into the election process. That will require a focused effort to find and elect legislators with the moral courage and mental capacity to act responsibly despite the deluge of money encouraging actions that may be contrary to the best interest of the country.

Another key factor in the Election Integrity discussion is the actual voting process. How is it managed? Do we really know who the voters are? Do voter registration records match the names of voters? Are the votes cast on time?

The list of questions can be extensive but they are legitimate questions that should be openly and honestly reviewed on a regular basis. For years, the election process had generally been considered fair and honest but uncertainty over election integrity has significantly increased over recent election cycles. Problems with traditional in-person election day voting have been minimal but questions surrounding absentee and mail-in voting have increased substantially. Some would have you believe mail-in voting is an open invitation to voter fraud despite dozens of subsequent investigations all reaching the same conclusion, no voter fraud found.

It's worth noting again that each state has its own regulations for how the voting process works in that particular state. Voting rules in some states may be more strict than in others, some more clearly written than in others. In my home state of Michigan, the voting process is well defined[6] for both in-person and absentee/mail-in ballots, although there is always room for improvement.

It's critically important these rules are regularly reviewed, updated as needed and are strictly enforced. Only then will we have confidence that every legitimate voter can vote confidentially and without inducement or fear of retribution, that all legitimate voters are granted reasonable access to voting places and that every citizen is entitled to cast only one vote in only one voting district.

LESSON THREE ☆ ☆ ☆
VOTER RESPONSIBILITY

Blaming politicians and political leaders for the problems in our country is a very common process, entertainment for some and a professional career for many others, especially those in the so called "news" business.

Some politicians have rightly earned public disdain based on their actions or inactions while in office. The majority of politicians are largely unknown, quietly plodding away doing just enough to get reelected next term. Thankfully, there is also a handful of very capable and committed legislators and officials dedicated to doing the right things and keeping us from being sucked beneath the surface and drowning in the ideological sewage pervasive across the Washington swamp. These legislators and officials are the lightning rods that attract the most attention and blame.

They are not the only participants in our democratic process. The voters elect the politicians. The politicians don't appoint themselves to office, although that may be debatable in some cases.

It is our responsibility as voters to assure that our democratic process works for the overall good of our country. Our current chaotic state is not the fault of the elected officials alone. We must make sound choices when we vote.

Obviously, that is not happening. Why not?

There can be many reasons. Consider the position the candidate is running for. The skills required for a competent legislator, whether representative or senator at federal or state level, are distinctly different than the skills needed for an executive position such as President or Governor or even City Mayors.

Legislators need to fully understand the wishes of those they represent. This requires the mental capacity to separate rational requests from the rantings of fringe elements or the emergency demands often fomented by mob mentality. This is not an easy task. Legislators need to learn how to listen. That's why you have two ears and only one mouth.

The legislator must be capable of crafting those voter wishes into clear, practical and realistic proposed laws. They of course will have staff available to do this with them or for them but the candidate must have the mental capacity to understand what the staff has presented.

All too often we see vague, half-baked proposed legislation or even fully enacted laws stuffed with garbage and lacking specificity, leaving it to the bureaucrats to figure out what was intended.

Worse yet are the monstrous two or three thousand-page bills cramming one or two legitimate, significant issues into a stew of political pork and campaign fantasies.

Wild-eyed, fire-breathing candidates overflowing with passion for their cause may not be the best choice as your legislative representative.

The skills and experiences required to become a competent President or Governor are distinctly different than those required for a legislator.

The positions of President or Governor are essentially executive positions. They are responsible for taking action in response to the real-time needs of their citizens/constituents. These positions require solid leadership skills, the ability to create effective management teams, to gather information and assess the circumstances quickly and to take decisive actions as required. And most importantly, to take responsibility for those actions.

There have been fourteen U.S. presidents since the end of WWII, Truman through Biden. Of those, eight had been former representatives

The Congressional Handbook

and/or senators in federal and/or state Legislatures. Of the remaining six presidents, four had no prior legislative experience but had held elected office as governors or vice presidents. Only two, Eisenhower and Trump, had never held elected office.

A quick recall of the country's economic performance and general sense of wellbeing under each of these presidents suggests an inverse relationship between presidential performance and legislative experience. The greater the amount of legislative experience, the worse the performance as president!

Electing the most qualified candidate should logically result in the best performance for our government and country. Candidates whose life experience consisted primarily as being a bartender or a community organizer (politically correct term for rabble rouser or shit disturber) or a lawyer may not have what it takes to be an effective leader.

A special note for those running for elected office. Make sure you have already achieved some sustainable, real-life experience before you run for office. You will need something to fall back on when you leave office, either on your own terms or by the legitimate vote of your constituents. Rational voters don't really care whether or not you get elected for a repeat term. If enough voters do not believe your performance has been acceptable, you will not get reelected. It could be a short legislative career!

Where do the candidates come from? How can we assure we have the best ones to choose from?

The election process in the U.S. is a state responsibility with each state setting its own election rules and managing its own election processes. All the states use some form of preliminary selection process to choose candidates that will be listed on the general election ballot. This applies for local, state or even federal elections although the federal election proces[s] is more complex.

The National Conference of State Legislatures[7] has summarized the preliminary candidate selection process or primary election that is managed by each state and can vary widely from state to state as outlined below:

CLOSED PRIMARIES: Voters must be a registered party member in order to participate in the candidate selection process in the nine states that have closed primaries.

PARTIALLY CLOSED PRIMARIES: Some states permit political parties to choose whether or not to allow unaffiliated voters to participate in their candidate selection process. This choice can change with each election cycle, leaving the political parties with maximum flexibility over who can vote in each Primary. Six states use the Partially Closed Primary system.

PARTIALLY OPEN PRIMARIES: Voters are permitted to cross party lines but must publicly declare their ballot choice and their ballot choice could be used as a form of voter registration for that party. Six states use this system.

OPEN to UNAFFILIATED VOTERS: Some states allow unaffiliated or independent voters to participate in any party primary they choose but voters who are registered with one party are not allowed to participate in another parties primary. Nine states use this voting system for their primary elections.

OPEN PRIMARIES: Typically, voters are not required to choose party affiliations when registering to vote. Voters can privately choose candidates from either party to fill a particular position or open seat. Voters can cast a vote across party lines for the primary election. Fifteen states use the open primary selection process.

OTHER PROCESSES: California and Washington use a top-two primary process with a common ballot listing all candidates, regardless of party affiliation. The top two candidates advance to the general election, regardless of party affiliation. Louisiana doesn't have a primary election. All candidates run on a single ticket on the general election date. If no candidate receives more than 50% of the vote, then a runoff election will be held six weeks later between the two candidates that got the highest and second highest number of votes. Nebraska elects legislators on a non-partisan basis from a single ballot with no party affiliation listed on the ballot. Alaska uses a top-four system for state and congressional offices.

PRESIDENTIAL PRIMARY RULES: Presidential primaries are an indirect candidate selection process. Each state has a number of party delegates that will attend the political party's nominating convention. The number of delegates and method of choosing delegates is managed by each political party.

In the presidential primary process, voters select the candidate of their choice and the delegates from each state vote accordingly for that candidate at the political party's nominating convention. A few states, notably Iowa, use a Caucus system controlled and managed by the political party to select their preferred candidate. Delegates from all the states then vote at the party's national convention to select their party's candidate to run nationwide for the office of President.

The way states handle their presidential primaries can vary significantly from their state primary processes. Some hold both primaries on the same day, others hold them weeks or months apart. Some hold state and presidential primaries on the same day but with different rules.

The rules for selecting candidates to run for political office are well defined but vary widely across the country. As a responsible voter, it is essential that you understand and participate in the primary election process in your state. If you don't like the way your state primary system works, you can always move to a state with a system more to your liking.

The lesson here is simple. Improving the performance of our government starts with electing better legislators and that requires having well-qualified candidates listed on the ballot for general elections. The primary process is a first step in this long journey. Failure to pay attention to the primary process can result in seriously flawed outcomes as we've seen in recent years.

LESSON FOUR ☆ ☆ ☆
THE PANDEMIC

Pandemic is a word that few people heard of until it burst onto the scene in early 2020. Suddenly the news was all about some dreaded pandemic, code named Covid-19. Panels of so-called experts appeared on every TV network to offer their opinions and expert advice. A White House Coronavirus Task Force (28 people) led by Vice President Mike Pence held daily press conferences to update the nation on the status of the pandemic.

What did all this mean? Will the pandemic have already faded away by the time this book is published?

Merriam-Webster defines pandemic as an outbreak of a disease that occurs over a wide geographic area (as multiple countries or continents) and typically affects a significant proportion of the population: a pandemic outbreak of a disease. Simply put, Covid-19 was bad and was spreading everywhere, but it wasn't the first time mankind has faced such a calamity.

The Bubonic Plague (Black Death) struck Europe during 1347 through 1351, killing an estimated 30 to 60 percent of the European population! Half of the people! Estimates vary but the plague might have reduced the total world population at that time from about 475 million down to between 350 and 375 million people. It took as many as two hundred years for the population to recover to pre-plague levels. Outbreaks of the plague recurred around the world until the early 19th century and small numbers of cases are reported annually[8] still today.

The Spanish Flu[9] (1918-1920) infected as many as 500 million people worldwide, which at the time was about a third of the earth's population. It's estimated that at least 50 million people died from that disease, with 675,000 deaths in the U.S. Based on the world's estimated population 1.86 billion[10] people in 1920, the calculated fatality rate for the Spanish flu was about 2.7%.

Today's pandemic, commonly referred to as Covid-19 or, depending on your sensitivities, the Wuhan Flu or even the China Virus, was first recognized in late 2019. It is still with us more than two years later. Based on recent breathless reports of the skyrocketing numbers of cases, you might think it is getting worse!

Let's get a grip on things.

World Health Organization (WHO) data shows there have been 5.5 million Covid-19-related deaths recorded worldwide as of the end of December 2021. At today's population of about 7.9 billion people, the Covid-19 global death rate is 0.07 percent, less than one tenth of one percent! While unacceptable at any level, the Covid-19 death rate is only 2.6% of the Spanish Flu rate and negligible compared to the Plague.

Some other comparisons give us even more reason to pause.

WHO data shows that global cancer deaths total roughly 10 million per year. Each year, cancer takes more lives than Covid-19 has taken over two years! Deaths from heart disease exceeded 17.9 million in 2019, more than three times the number of Covid-19-related deaths to date. Granted, Covid-19 is not over yet and the total number of victims will continue to rise. It's also a particularly virulent virus which has been difficult if not impossible to contain. But it is far less disastrous than some prior pandemics and has killed far fewer people than die annually from other diseases we live with every day.

So why are we devoting so much of our time, emotional effort and money in a seemingly futile attempt to get control of this virus?

Using the time-tested analysis technique of Follow the Money or in this case, Follow the Power, could be helpful. To understand problems in

America, look at who profits from that problem, not who suffers from it. Who benefits from keeping Covid-19 the leading story?

Obviously the mainstream TV news media is one benefactor. Every hour can include multiple stories on the progress or lack thereof in combating the disease. An endless number of people with widely varying degrees of expertise and competence are eager to get on TV and experience their two minutes of fame.

Some of the experts have gone to great lengths to maximize their exposure across as many media platforms as possible including so-called exclusive interviews and Sunday morning talk show appearances. This approach seems especially appealing to those formerly unheard of minions who worked for years in the bowels of Washington's mind-numbing bureaucracy but have now been elevated to the lofty heights which they so justly deserve. At least in their opinion.

Politicians also benefit from continuing the Covid-19 frenzy. If you are a member of the party currently in power, you can wring your hands and feel the pain of your constituents. You can wax poetically about all the plans your party is making to combat this deadly disease. Whether or not those plans make any sense is quite irrelevant, you have a great talking point.

Covid-19 also provides great cover for failed policies in other parts of government. Keeping the Covid-19 pot boiling will surely draw attention away from other government policy blunders.

How do they keep the pot boiling? It's all in the numbers. When things start to settle down, along comes a new variant such as the Omicron variant, providing a fresh opportunity to crank out endless reports of new, exploding numbers of cases. Limited mention of severity levels or numbers of deaths, just the rapidly expanding number of cases. Even murkier, no access to the number of deaths caused by Covid-19 vs. number of deaths where Covid-19 was present but not the cause of death. Think about a person suffering severe injuries in a car crash. While in intensive care at the hospital, it's discovered the victim also has Covid-19. The victim dies the next day. How is that recorded in the Covid data?

There are many very important lessons to be learned from this Covid-19 tragedy.

Maybe the greatest has come from exposing the public to the true depths of the "never let a good crisis go to waste" doctrine first credited to Winston Churchill in the mid-1940s. A prime example of this is the foolhardy closing of schools and the mandated wearing of masks to protect students with no consideration for the impact on the students and with virtually no data suggesting closures or mask wearing would have any impact on Covid-19.

School administrations and unions score 5 points, students score 0 points.

The next part of this lesson is about dealing with Covid reality. Instead of spouting bold slogans like "two weeks to slow the spread" or "shut down the virus, not the country," ask yourself if enough attention was focused on possible cures.

Early efforts were loudly mocked by mainstream media and the talking heads. Ill-conceived measures such as lockdowns, social distancing, mask mandates and other theatrical actions were much more politically attractive and assured higher media ratings.

Was any consideration given to the possibility that Mother Nature, or Nature's Birthing Person for those of you stricken with wokism, is difficult if not impossible to beat?

Finally, lessons for politicians and other wannabe leaders. Don't shoot first and ask questions later. When disaster strikes, try to get straight answers from verifiable, credible sources before spouting platitudes. Don't make stupid promises, no matter how well intended they may be. Video recordings and emails never go away.

Most important is the lesson for the voters. Does your candidate have what it takes to rationally handle a crisis? Has the candidate ever had any crisis experience? Any real leadership experience? As a voter, are you yourself capable of managing through difficult times? You may well need to be if you elected the wrong candidate.

LESSON FIVE ☆ ☆ ☆
EMERGENCY POWERS

One good thing has emerged from the Covid-19 pandemic. The general public has discovered the serious flaws in the emergency powers regulations that currently exist in many of our states.

These emergency powers regulations were originally enacted to provide temporary authority for governors to take extraordinary actions to maintain order and protect citizens in extreme and unforeseen circumstances. Coping with natural disasters resulting from hurricanes, tornadoes, forest fires or other environmental extremes are an obvious reason for granting such emergency powers. Likewise, dire circumstances enabled by humans such as chemical spills, industrial explosions, or extreme civil unrest resulting in riots are also obvious reasons for granting such emergency powers.

These various emergency powers acts were applied from time to time as originally intended and went largely unnoticed until the early spring of 2020. That's when the full impact of the Covid-19 pandemic began to emerge. People across the nation suddenly discovered the enormous power that had been granted to state governors under the various emergency powers acts. In many cases, power that was outside the control or influence of the state's duly elected legislators.

Some governors handled this power responsibly.

Others did not.

With virtually no precedent in any free society, and only limited and questionable science supporting their actions, these governors reacted to Covid-19 in a kneejerk manner, taking extraordinary steps in the name of public safety by shutting down the economy in their state and imprisoning us in the confines of our homes. Some even suggested imposing restrictions on how we behaved inside our own private homes. I wonder how they intended to police that.

Rational people saw this as a massive power grab, the first step towards tyranny. Others, like lost sheep, blindly followed the rules in the name of public safety, paralyzed with the fear spread by the ratings' hungry mainstream news media.

Some of the governors, flush with this newly acquired power, saw themselves as the next Messiah, saviors of the masses and surely destined for greatness.

At least, that's what it looked like. The situation in Michigan was particularly instructive.

On March 10, 2020, Michigan's Governor Whitmer issued an Executive Order number 2020-4 declaring a statewide declaration of emergency due to Covid-19. This order was issued under The Emergency Powers of Governor Act of 1945 and the Emergency Management Act 390 of 1976. Executive Order 2020-4 paved the way for the governor to institute massive and ill-advised intrusions into the daily lives of Michigan's residents. Selected businesses were arbitrarily shut down, masking and social distancing mandates were issued, schools were closed, public and even private gatherings were restricted and society in general was put under the thumb of the governor.

Congers up visions of the days of Emperors and Monarchs.

Where was the Michigan legislature? They were responding, trying to instill reason and curb the powers of the governor. Michigan had a divided government with the Republicans holding the majority in both the Senate and House of Representatives while the governor was a Democrat. The legislatures wanted the economy reopened and the most egregious

Covid-19 restrictions lifted. The governor was not interested in giving up power but there was hope.

The Emergency Measures Act included a time limit. After 28 days, the governor was required to declare the emergency terminated[11] unless both houses of the legislature requested an extension of the state of emergency. The governor found a clever way around this. As the end of the 28-day period approached, Governor Whitmer simply redeclared the same state of emergency, issued a new executive order and rescinded the prior emergency order. This went on for several months with only the occasional minor relaxing of restrictions by the Monarch of Michigan. The legislature passed a law limiting the governor's emergency powers. The governor vetoed that legislation. Lawsuits were filed against the governor's actions. The case went through the court system, eventually reaching the Michigan Supreme Court, which determined the governor's actions were unconstitutional and therefore invalid.

Suddenly, under the Michigan Health Code authority, the Michigan Department of Health and Human Services issued orders reinstating most of the same restrictions that had just been struck down by the state Supreme Court.

You can't make this stuff up.

Meanwhile, organizations had been collecting signatures for ballot initiatives to shift uncontrolled power away from the governor. Under Michigan law, such citizen-initiated measures can be voted and approved by both houses of the legislature and then implemented without the governor's signature. The initiatives were veto-proof.

In July of 2021, the 76-year-old Emergency Power of Governor Act 302 of 1945 was officially repealed. The emperor's wings were clipped. It had taken roughly 16 months for this to play out, 16 months of political overreach and severe social and economic harm to the communities and citizens of Michigan.

Many other states were (some still are) similarly harmed by the excesses of their political leaders during the pandemic, although perhaps with less theatrics than we saw here in Michigan (former governor Cuomo in New York deserves honorable mention).

What's the lesson here?

Power can be addictive, especially political power which can have such significant influence and control over ordinary people. Those with political power also find it easy to attract adoring crowds willing to do almost anything to keep their political leader in power. At its extremes, this power can be a great benefit to a nation and its people (Franklin D. Roosevelt, Donald J. Trump) or could lead to disastrous results (Adolf Hitler, Fidel Castro).

How can we protect ourselves from these extremes?

First, pay close attention to what's really going on. Why are the leaders making emergency changes to the rules? Is there a real threat (if the wind is blowing 100 mph and the rain is teaming down by the bucket full, it's probably a real threat) or is it just a forecast threat based on some fuzzy study (temperatures will rise by 1 degree in ten years unless we stop eating beef—kill the cows). Was locking down the country for "two weeks to flatten the curve" well thought out?

Probably the most critical issue is defining exactly how the emergency ends. What are the specific rules for declaring the emergency ended and the emergency powers no longer valid? Michigan's law outlined a thirty-day limit on the Governor's emergency power but the Monarch of Michigan found a way to work around that. You've got to think these things through using the widest range of inputs you can find. Don't listen only to the mainstream media or the chattering class, they may already be under the spell. Carefully evaluate whether you will be better off if these emergency changes and rules are enacted.

You have to stand up for your rights, otherwise they will disappear. Vote!

LESSON SIX ☆ ☆ ☆
EXPIRATION DATES

We have far too many politicians who have never been anything but a politician for most of their careers. Some have been in office for half a century or longer, still showing no signs of having a credible exit plan.

If you keep milk or eggs past their best by dates, they get sour and then turn rotten. Same with fresh fruit. One apple or pear turns bad and next thing you know, the whole basket is rotten. Same thing in Congress.

This begs the question, should we have term limits for members of Congress?

Term limits have been established for the office of the President of the United States. Likewise, many states have term limits for their governors and some state legislators are also term limited. If it's appropriate for the president and governors, why not for Congress?

Commercial airline pilots are typically required to retire at age 65, based on an assumed age-related degradation in capabilities making them a potential safety risk. Should we have the same concerns about our congressional legislators? Do their capabilities decline with age and if so, is that also a safety risk or a risk to the security of our nation or even a risk to our economy?

The National Conference of State Legislatures (NCSL) reports in the years 1990 through 2000 a total of twenty-one states enacted term limits for their legislatures. During that same period, six states repealed their term limits either through legislative action or state Supreme Court rulings. Today, fifteen states still have some form of term limits for their legislators. Have these term limits been effective? Has the legislative performance or stability improved in these states? The NCSL published an article by Karl Kurtz, Feb. 8, 2021, which reviews the impact of term limits in several states. The results are mixed at best.

Studies showed turnover rates increased in legislatures with term limits vs. those without term limits. Some say that's a good thing. Others point out the loss of experienced leadership in these legislatures, especially in key roles such as committee chairmanships and house speaker positions. This has resulted in weakening the legislative branch relative to the power of the governor's office. Was this a factor in some of the colossal screwups we saw during the Covid-19 pandemic?

Governors in many states are also subject to term limits but the impact seems to have been minimal. The governors continue to have large staffs plus access to and authority over the state agencies filled with well-experienced bureaucrats. Even with term limits, the legislatures still come out on the short end of the power balance. Fifteen states have had legislative term limits in place for about thirty years now and whether effective or not, these states have generally learned to live with these restrictions. There are no indications these states are any better or worse off than states without term limits.

The question of age limits or expiration dates is a separate issue that is still being debated. A Washington Post article on June 2, 2021, notes at the beginning of 2021, the average age of the U.S. Senators was 64.3 years, the oldest Senate in U.S. history. President Harry S. Truman reportedly wrote a note indirectly suggesting strong support for age limits: "Twelve years of Washington is enough for any man. We'd help cure senility, and seniority—both terrible legislative diseases."

Setting age limits would be a very difficult task. People develop, mature and decline at different rates. Many of us know people who continue to perform at very high levels well into their 80s and 90s. We also know many who have declined, sometimes rapidly starting in their 50s or even earlier. Can we come up with a fair and logical test to determine continued eligibility for office? Commercial pilots can be put through rigorous tests in flight simulators to measure and assess their piloting skills. What tests or measurements would we use for politicians? The number of TV interviews they've had in the past 12 months? The number of legislative bills they authored that became law? The total dollars' worth of programs they brought home to their districts, regardless of whether the programs had any real value? Should we award them bonus points for not being exposed in any scandals?

You can see the problem.

Once again, the answer is up to the legitimate voters in each district. Use the smell test, same as you do when you pour a glass of milk. If it doesn't smell right you throw it out. If your political candidate isn't performing as you would expect or the candidate's promises or actions don't seem quite right, throw the bum out.

LESSON SEVEN ☆ ☆ ☆
CLIMATE CHANGE

I lived near Niagara Falls in the late 1960s and witnessed firsthand the birth of what has become today's Climate Change religion. Back then it was known as the Anti-Pollution movement, a term that accurately described the significant environmental issues at the time. Two of the Great Lakes, Lake Erie and Lake Ontario, were effectively dead from the combination of raw sewage and industrial waste being dumped into those lakes. The southern portion of Lake Michigan had similar challenges for the same reasons due to the large population of the greater Chicago region plus the heavy industrial developments along the shoreline in northeastern Illinois and northern Indiana. Similar situations existed in many of the heavily populated and highly industrialized parts of the world.

In our case, the negative impacts were obvious. Dead fish along the shorelines of the Great Lakes. Layers of industrial haze hanging over the steel plants and chemical refineries. Sickly orange and yellowish froth dumping out of open drain pipes from factories and paper mills directly into the rivers and streams. You could see one such huge drainage tunnel emptying straight into the Niagara River gorge just a couple hundred yards from the famous Niagara Falls.

I supported the movement as did many other young people and early onset "Greenies" at the time. Anti-pollution legislation was passed and in a remarkably short time the lakes recovered, the air cleared up and the froth disappeared from the streams.

And then what happened?

The anti-pollution legislation resulted in the creation of new government agencies in many countries, notably the Environmental Protection Agency (EPA) in the U.S. The fatal flaw in this legislation, as in most legislation, was the lack of an exit plan. What to do when the mission had been accomplished? There was no sunset provision.

All these anti-pollution bureaucrats rather liked their jobs, their steady government paychecks and virtually guaranteed lifetime employment but needed a reason for continuing with their assignments. So they decided if progress had been made by tightening up environmental regulations, tightening them even more should make things get even better. Thus began the downward spiral of ever-increasing environmental regulations with little or no regard to possible negative consequences. Regulatory changes were made from somewhere deep within the bureaucracy with little or no legislative oversight or authority.

The term "anti-pollution" wasn't broad enough to capture the expanding aims of this bureaucratic juggernaut so global warming became the catch phrase. After a few years it was discovered that Mother Nature was not cooperating and the actual global temperatures weren't going up fast enough to support this new rhetoric.

Now what do we do?

A new phrase, Climate Change, is born. What a brilliant solution! The climate is always changing, day to day, year to year, and has been for millions of years. Sometimes hotter, sometimes colder, wetter, drier, and on and on. So now we have the Religion of Climate Change which cannot be dislodged by mere logic or measurement since climate always has and always will change. They had it made, the EPA and like organizations around the world. They could have been comfortably employed for generations, monitoring the weather, writing papers and attending global conferences on the evils of Climate Change.

But that was not flashy enough, didn't create enough headlines or

The Congressional Handbook

provide enough leverage to launch personal or political power trips. Now we have to STOP Climate Change. What makes us think the climate is not supposed to change? Breathless claims of "The world is going to end in 12 years if we don't address climate change," says NY-DM Rep. Ocasio-Cortez in January 2019.

We are three years into that dire warning and still counting.

Almost ten years earlier, in December 2009, former vice president Al Gore was quoting (inaccurately) research indicating "Some of the (climate) models suggest there is a 75% chance that the entire north polar ice cap during some of the summer months could be completely ice free within the next five to seven years." That target date passed more than five years ago and you can still walk across the North Pole in the summertime.

Who says temperatures shouldn't rise like they have for the last 50,000 years? Ice ages come and go in cycles with numerous studies and scientific articles suggesting the earth has experienced five or more such cycles in the last four hundred and fifty thousand years.[12] Temperatures will fall again. When they start to fall again, how far should we let them fall? Who decides? That same "scientific" community that's been guiding us through the Covid pandemic?

The Climate Change crowd continues to blame us mere humans for all the environmental calamities we supposedly face today. History shows that natural catastrophes have inflicted far more environmental harm than anything man has caused.

On August 26, 1883, an Indonesian island named Krakatau exploded[13] and disappeared from the face of the earth. This volcanic eruption remains the largest eruption ever recorded, killing an estimated 35,000 people, setting off tidal waves greater than 120 feet high and sending millions of tons of ash and gases as much as 50 miles up into the atmosphere. Global temperatures dropped by 0.5 degree C in the following year and did not return to normal until 1888, five years later.

But temperatures did return to normal. Life naturally accommodated, adapted and recovered, just as it has for eons. Evolution has been around for quite some time, even longer than some politicians. We see lots of articles about the extinction of various species of plants, animals and birds, especially about those little critters that are often used to halt all sorts of manmade projects and activities. Yet we rarely see reports of the discovery of new species or the constantly evolving plant and animal life that's happening around us every day. Those reports just aren't sensational enough for today's audiences. Catastrophes yes, reality no.

If you are running for office or are involved with any of the myriad of federal, state and local agencies that deal with various aspects of the EPA or related regulations, please take a deep breath and try to think clearly about your environmental beliefs. Are you a stopper, bent on bringing progress and development to a halt, or are you an adapter, capable of seeing beyond the noise and able to craft policies and solutions enabling us to adapt to the realities of the world?

Talk with your constituents about their environmental concerns. Make sure you get a complete and balanced story. Shutting down dirty coal mines and power plants sounds nice but what are the real costs of replacement energy? The wind doesn't always blow, the sun doesn't always shine and batteries are full of really nasty stuff.

We all want safe, clean water, clear air, pristine landscapes. How clean is clean? How clear is clear? Pristine? I'll bet Manhattan Island was really pristine 500 years ago! Should we eliminate New York City?

What's the lesson here?

The climate is going to change regardless of human intervention. Enacting rational EPA regulations limiting severe abuses to the environment is a noble and appropriate activity. But the regulations must be reasonable. Overall we must learn to live with climate change, evolve with it and benefit from its changes.

LESSON EIGHT ☆ ☆ ☆
ACCOUNTABILITY

Accountability. One of the most contradictory words in the English language.

When used by voters or the general public, accountability typical means getting politicians or government officials to accept responsibility for actions they've taken (or not taken). This applies to everything from creating new legislation to implementing and abiding by current laws and regulations or to the way they conduct their professional and personal affairs. Voters elect politicians to represent them. Voters expect those politicians to take responsibility for their actions and for the results they produce.

Politicians see it differently, viewing accountability as a binary choice either claiming responsibility for success, or blaming others for failure. If a particular action or policy position is popular and broadly accepted by the media and the general public, the politician will quickly and loudly claim responsibility for its success. You often see this soon after an election, especially if the party in power has changed. Politicians will claim credit for an improving economy even though that improvement was likely due to changes made by the prior government months or even years earlier.

However, if a particular action or policy is not popular or goes terribly wrong, the politician immediately denies any responsibility. They insulate themselves even further with demands for a review "We've got to get to the bottom of this," followed quickly by "We've got to hold them accountable!" Notice how it's always "them" that must be held accountable.

Why do we always need to get to the bottom of this? Why don't the guilty just admit what they did and take responsibility for it? That never seems to happen in politics. Do they really think it will just all go away? Yes, that is exactly what they think and for good reason. It often does just go away! It gets buried so far down within the bureaucracy that it never sees the light of day (ergo the term Foggy Bottom).

Reports of UFO sightings circulated for well over 50 years but the U.S. Government never admitted it had evidence of such sightings until last year[14] (2021). Rumors circulated for years about the existence of a mysterious military operation located in Nevada known as Area 51. The U.S. government through all its various agencies including the military flatly denied such rumors with that contemptuous move-on, nothing-to-see-here wave-off. Now we know operations at Area 51 began in 1955 but remained completely under wraps until August 2013, when a CIA Report written in 1992 was declassified and released in response to a FOIA request issued in 2005.[15]

Let that sink in. It took eight years to declassify and release a report that was by then 21 years old, about a program that was initiated 37 years before that! The mind boggles.

One can understand needing such strict secrecy for issues of national security and the development of very advanced, cutting-edge technologies.

Do those same burial procedures apply to more mundane issues? Will we ever know why U.S. Ambassador J.C. Stevens was executed in Benghazi in 2012? Why was he in Benghazi anyway? It's not even the capitol of Libya! His security detachment called for additional help but reinforcements were not sent! Why didn't they go to help? Who called them off? What are the chances we will ever learn the truth about that incident?

Verification is another troubling aspect when it comes to political accountability. If the "truth" ever does surface, it's often represented in documents or reports with significant portions heavily redacted (fancy term for blacked out) making it virtually impossible to understand. The Freedom of Information Act (FOIA) allows redaction for nine specific situations or "exemptions"[16] plus three "exclusions." Not surprising, the exemptions and exclusions are broad enough to drive a truck through!

It gets even murkier (the deeper you go the foggier it gets). The OPEN Government Act[17] (Openness Promotes Effectiveness in our National Government Act) was passed in 2007 to clarify and enhance some parts of the FOIA legislation, including statements noting why specific redactions were applied in any documents released by the government.

How clever. They've clarified how to redact[18] so you know why you can't know! Is it any wonder why people are suspicious of governments?

To all those current and future legislators, government officials and bureaucrats, accountability is a really simple concept.

As a legislator, all you need to do is demonstrate your willingness to be judged by others on your actual performance.

Voters don't get a free pass either. When it comes to accountability, voters are the ones who keep reelecting the underperformers and scoundrels. Andrew Cuomo was in his third term as governor when his past finally caught up with him. Although Trump had no prior political experience or related baggage, there was considerable negative press covering his years in the property development business. History will judge whether voters won or lost that election gamble. At the end of Biden's first year in office, polls suggested voters were already feeling considerable remorse.

If voters keep electing representatives or senators or governors with cloudy histories, why should we expect better results? Human nature being what it is, the probability of achieving increased transparency and accountability in politics and government anytime soon seems very unlikely.

LESSON NINE ☆ ☆ ☆
CONCENTRATION OF POWER

Looking at voting patterns and election results over the years, I've always been curious why large, heavily populated cities tend to vote Democrat. As you move farther from these densely populated areas, the voting tends to favor Republican candidates. Another way of looking at it shows voters along the Atlantic coastline and the Pacific coastline favor one party while inland states and counties favor the other party. Is there some correlation between political views and population density? Does the presence of ocean currents or proximity to saltwater impact election results? What really happens when you concentrate people, or power, or just about anything?

It turns out really bad things can happen. The atomic bomb explodes by squeezing a bunch of uranium together into a concentrated mass very quickly. The results are disastrous.

Normal, everyday products can also become lethal. It all depends on the concentration level or dosage[19].

If you consumed 33 tubes of toothpaste, it would kill you.

If you consumed 78 shots of espresso, it would kill you.

Only 13 shots of alcohol produces same effect.

Water. Plain, everyday water. Drink 6 liters quickly—you die!

So how many politicians or bureaucrats concentrated together does it take to kill your ideas, your hopes and dreams, your communities (defund the police) or the economy (Covid lockdowns)?

Consider the high numbers of politicians and bureaucrats concentrated in and around Washington, D.C. An organization chart from the United States Government Manual, 2002 shows the layout and reporting structure of the U.S. Government. The U.S. Constitution is at the top of the chart with the three co-equal branches, Legislative, Executive and Judicial next in line. Within each are several separate Offices or Councils or various levels of Courts in the case of the Judicial Branch. The U.S. Botanical Garden is listed under the Legislative Branch. Who knew they had a green thumb!

The remainder of the chart shows the massive tangle of departments and various organizations that report directly to the Executive Branch of our government. There are fifteen different cabinet level departments such as Agriculture, Labor, Transport, etc., each one headed by a Cabinet Secretary and each stuffed with monstrous layers of bureaucracies within them.

Providing effective leadership and direction of fifteen large and complex departments, including the military, is a daunting task. But it doesn't end there. Another fifty-eight agencies, separate from and in addition to the fifteen cabinet-level departments, are shown reporting directly to the Executive Branch. These fifty-eight agencies are listed under the heading "Independent Establishments and Government Corporations."

Think about that for a moment. Fifteen cabinet-level departments, each headed by a cabinet secretary and each with several deputy secretary positions reporting to them. Add in countless numbers of nauseating, elitist bureaucrats in charge of their own little fiefdoms within the department, you know, the ones we saw starring (sorry, I meant testifying) in the numerous congressional theater performances (sorry again, congressional hearings) we've seen over the past few years. Then consider the fifty-eight independent agencies, many virtually unknown to the general public, each headed by someone with a fancy tile and a sizable staff (except maybe the Office of Government Ethics, which is either under staffed or highly incompetent).

The Congressional Handbook

All of this can easily add to thousands of people all vying for attention from the Executive Office of the President. They can't all be accommodated so what do they do? They talk to each other. They form little groups or alliances and come up with fanciful ideas to satisfy their need for attention. I suspect many of these fanciful ideas mysteriously appear as revised regulations, all created without adult supervision or legislative oversight.

It's easy to see how this can happen. Currently, the Federal Register or United States Code allegedly consists of over 200 volumes (does anybody know for sure) and is expanding with the addition of new rules and regulations at the rate of 90,000 pages per year! You can imagine how totally wacky concepts could creep in as new regulations and nobody would know until it's too late. By any measure, this is a degree of concentration of power well past the toxic level.

How do we regain control?

Most of these Departments and Independent Establishments are based in Washington, D.C., or the immediate surrounding suburbs. Why not spread them out across the country? Reduce the concentration and therefore the toxicity level.

Let's put the FBI in Chicago, near one of the highest crime and corruption centers in America.

How about Department of Energy in Houston or Tulsa or Wyoming or even West Virginia?

Health and Welfare to Rochester, MN, or Baltimore or Cleveland?

Department of Agriculture—Kansas City or Des Moines?

Department of Education—just disband it completely, it's a State responsibility!

Department of State—move it to Fairbanks, right next door to Russia and China.

Department of Transport—Toledo, Ohio

EPA—Fargo, North Dakota (minimal global warming impact)

Homeland Security—Eagle Pass, TX, or Tucson, AZ, or maybe Bangor,

39

Maine (all are closer to borders than Washington, D.C.).

FEMA—New Orleans

Drug Enforcement Administration—San Francisco

You get the point, put them closer to the issues they should be dealing with.

The only ones left in D.C. should be the IRS (nobody else wants them), Justice (to watch the members of Congress) and the military (so we can all watch them).

While the logic of reducing concentration or decentralizing government is inescapable, the likelihood of it happening is limited. The catering industry in D.C. would collapse without all those suck-up cocktail parties! The lobbyists would have to disperse their operations all across the country.

And what about all those unemployable elitist experts and bureaucrats who will become unemployed because they were afraid to move out of the D.C. bubble and live in the real world with the people they supposedly work for.

Voters need to think carefully about the impact of population density and how living in urban communities might shape your political views. Are you voting on your own terms or are you following the crowd? Beware of mob rule.

The Congressional Handbook

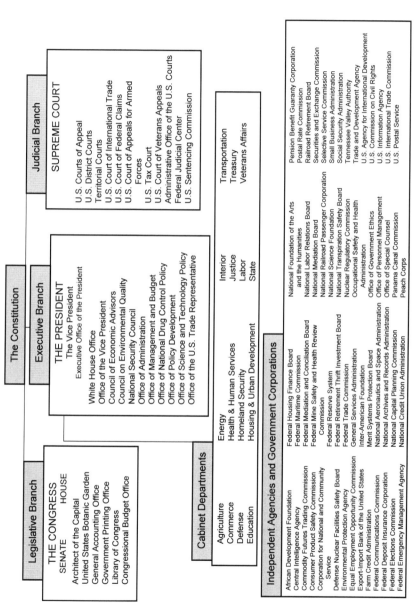

Figure 3.1 Organizational Chart for the United States Federal Government
Source: *United States Government Manual*, 2002. The chart has been updated to reflect Homeland Security.

LESSON TEN ☆ ☆ ☆
SOCIAL JUSTICE

One of the most ill-defined concepts of our time is the issue of Social Justice. A term spewed from the mouths of self-important politicians, academics, insufferable bureaucrats, community organizers, mainstream media's talking heads and other ne'er-do-wells. All in breathless support of this concept.

In support of what? What does Social Justice actually mean?

Here are some definitions pulled randomly from the center of all knowledge, the Internet:

Definition from Oxford Languages

so·cial jus·tice

noun

justice in terms of the distribution of wealth, opportunities, and privileges within a society.

"individuality gives way to the struggle for social justice"

Definition from The San Diego Foundation

What is meant by Social Justice?

"Social justice is the view that everyone deserves equal economic, political and social rights and opportunities. Social workers aim to open the doors of access and opportunity for everyone, particularly those in greatest need."

National Association of Social Workers. "Social justice encompasses economic justice." Mar. 24, 2016

Definition of Social Justice - John Lewis Institute:

Social justice is a communal effort dedicated to creating and sustaining a fair and equal society in which each person and all groups are valued and affirmed. It encompasses efforts to end systemic violence and racism and all systems that devalue the dignity and humanity of any person. It recognizes that the legacy of past injustices remains all around us, so therefore promotes efforts to empower individual and communal action in support of restorative justice and the full implementation of human and civil rights. Social justice imperatives also push us to create a civic space defined by universal education and reason and dedicated to increasing democratic participation.

In all of these explanations, there is no mention of personal responsibility and no reference to family, two of the most basic foundations of civil society.

Several years ago I bought a book titled A Theory of Justice by John Rawls, first published in 1971. It is a mind-numbing 587-page tomb, an almost incomprehensible compilation of academic drivel, rife with delusional conclusions drawn from imaginary studies of people each hidden behind a veil of secrecy, thus insuring their thoughts are pure and not sullied by reality. That published work was regarded by many as the benchmark for the modern-day Social Justice movement.

During my college days, about the same time the Rawls book was written, I recall many late-night sessions at my fraternity house where we developed far more realistic and sustainable social theories, usually after returning from serious fluid dynamics study sessions at Sports Bar & Grill.

You can spend hours combing through the mountains of information on Social Justice available via the Internet. Much of it is well intentioned and occasionally includes well-reasoned positions on very complex social issues. Much of it is also garbage, unvarnished trash designed primarily to incent unrest and civil disobedience.

The premise of today's Social Justice boils down to: Everything seems to be someone else's fault and all can be rectified by some institutional (government) action or policy. If we just stick together as a group, someone will take care of us.

For the past ten years or more, all the above definitions have talked of basic equality amongst and across all people, including equality of access and opportunity for all. More recently, a new term has crept into the Social Justice concept. People now talk of "equity" instead of "equality." What's the difference?

Equality is about treating individuals the same no matter their group identity.

Equity is about treating individuals differently based on their group identity to achieve equal group outcomes.[20]

The Social Justice warriors don't seem happy with equal opportunity, the chance for all to do their individual best to achieve their personal hopes and dreams. Instead they want assurance of equal outcomes for particular groups. This supposedly will be achieved by providing different inputs or special advantages to preferred groups, depending on that groups perceived needs.

Sounds eerily familiar, "from each according to his ability, to each according to his needs" (Karl Marx, 1875). That system as proposed by Marx has been tried many times around the world over the past two centuries and the outcome has always been the same. Complete and utter failure. Why would anybody want to try it again?

To those current and potential future Representatives, Senators and others entrusted to represent us, please understand the difference between equality and equity. Failure to distinguish between the two will be catastrophic.

If you look a bit deeper into the principles and issues within Social Justice, you will often see the term reparations, or more subtly restorative justice related to past injustices. What does this really mean? In its most basic terms, it means you white people need to pay us because some of your forefathers owned slaves more than 150 years ago.

Yes, there was slavery in this country in the past. It was wrong then and it is wrong now. It ended in this country many generations ago. It still exists in places around the world today, predominately Africa, Asia and the Middle East in various forms including entrapment, sex trafficking and domestic servitude.

But let's focus on the U.S. and the potential impacts of a reparations program.

First, who qualifies to receive compensation? Is it just blacks who can prove one or more of their ancestors was a slave? What about all the Chinese who were brought to this country as forced labor to build the railroads in the late 1800s?

Who pays? Just those unlucky white descendants of slave owners? How do you prove their forefathers were slave owners? How much do they pay? Should it vary depending on the conditions of slavery? Is the compensation the same if the slave was the butler for a wealthy family and lived in relative comfort vs. the compensation for a cotton picker or other manual laborer who presumably lived in substandard conditions, maybe even brutalized by his owner?

Why penalize the slave owner who was just the last person on the slave trade chain? Why not go back to the person that captured the slave in the first place, taking them from their native home in Africa and selling them to the trader who marched them to the holding areas waiting for the ships to arrive? What about the owners of those slave ships or their captains or crew members?

It's important to recognize that the alleged slave owners (white Americans) did not capture the slaves. They were captured by black tribal leaders and warlords. I've traveled along parts of coastal Africa and have seen remains of the slave-trading forts and holding areas. Discussions with local businessmen and transportation authorities indicate it was black

The Congressional Handbook

tribesmen who brought freshly captured slaves to these ports and slave docks for sale to the shippers. White men didn't capture the slaves, they would have been massacred before they got five miles inland from the coast.

One could make the case that those who arrived in America as slaves were the lucky ones. They had value for the plantation owners and were fed and housed at levels that would maintain their value. Had they not been brought to America, they may well have been captured in battles or kidnapped and enslaved or even slaughtered in the never-ending tribal wars or died from starvation or disease. These conditions still exist in parts of Africa today. Many of those currently calling for reparations might only exist because their predecessors were American slaves.

As you can see, the issues are very complex. Suggesting they can be resolved through reparations is unworkable.

To those who aspire to a seat in Congress, please be aware of the dangers inherent in promoting or enacting policies without full and due consideration of all sides of an issue.

LESSON ELEVEN ☆ ☆ ☆
MUDDLED THINKING

Anyone looking at our federal government today would be hard-pressed to say they are an example of efficiency or a fine-tuned operation. Many state governments and local city governments especially in the larger urban areas fall under this same affliction. In the worst case they are complete dysfunctional disasters, in the most generous case they would be considered "muddled."

Definitions from Oxford Languages shows "muddled" as a state of bewildered or bewildering confusion or disorder. Fits pretty well with what we see today. Our governments are an unmistakable reflection of our society, truly a product of our election results. Do you ever recall your parents saying be careful what you wish for? The same logic should apply to voting.

If we are not vigilant, muddled thinking can and occasionally does creep into our laws and regulations. Some examples of muddled thinking are shown below.

CANCEL CULTURE

One of the most absurd concepts that has surfaced over the past few years is a spinoff from old-fashioned mob mentality into what's now called cancel culture. It's the adolescent version of a five-year-old sticking their fingers in their ears and screaming, "No, nooh, nooohhhh," when faced with a choice they don't like.

The idea that you can get whatever you want by simply yelling louder and longer has worked for politicians, union leaders, academics and elitists from time to time in the past. But now it has been taken to a new, very disturbing level.

The cancel culture crowd takes offense at anything and everything they even remotely disagree with. They demand their colleagues as well as the general public stop associating with or doing business with anyone who doesn't share their opinion. The intended result is social starvation and economic castration of the offending party.

Far too many people including mainline media personalities, entertainers, sports stars and tragically, many large corporate leaders succumb to these schoolyard bullying tactics.

It is way past time for the legislators, the parents and the voters to just say no to cancel culture.

CRIME REDUCTION

Violent crime has been increasing at an alarming rate across many areas of the U.S. in recent years. This includes armed robberies, organized smash and grab shopping sprees, random acts of violence such as driving an SUV at high speed into a holiday parade or pushing people off subway platforms into the path of an oncoming commuter train, gang wars with dozens of people shot and killed each week in larger cities and the all-too-frequent mass shootings in schools or other public places.

People are sick and tired of all this senseless violence and are demanding action from their political leaders.

There seems to be only one common response, gun reform! If we just get rid of the guns this will all go away, shout the politicians, the mainstream media, the academics and the elitists. Repeal or neutralize the Second Amendment!

Despite the vociferous claims of many conservatives and gun rights supporters, the Second Amendment does not give the people of this country the right to have and use guns. Instead the Second Amendment specifically prohibits the government from taking that right away from the people. "...,the right of the people to keep and bear Arms shall not be infringed."

People have the natural right to protect themselves from all types of danger including natural events like fire and floods or from intruders like wild animals or other humans and possibly the most dangerous intruder of all, our own government!

Politicians jump on the gun control bandwagon because it is a simple, easy-to-grasp concept that fits neatly into the soundbite culture of our times. Looking at the root causes for increasing crime requires a lot of time and in-depth analysis. Politicians want something to say right now, while the particular catastrophe is still right in front of everyone in the news. A week from now the country will have moved on to some other flashy issue of the day.

The root causes for the current crime wave are many and varied. The breakdown of traditional family and community values are a factor. High incarceration rates in inner cities brought on to a great extent by prior political solutions (war on drugs laws enacted in the 90s) directly contribute to the breakdown of the family and community system. Identity politics plays a destabilizing role by ensuring there is always someone else to blame instead of taking personal responsibility for one's actions.

Public safety is the primary responsibility of all levels of government, national, state and local. Rising criminal activity is a complex problem with no easy "one size fits all" solution. Long-term solutions must include recognizing and dealing effectively with mental health issues, drug abuse issues and socioeconomic issues combined with solid law enforcement practices. Guns are only a tool used in crimes, not the cause of the crime.

Voters need to understand this and select candidates capable of crafting real-world, workable solutions for reducing crime.

FREE STUFF

The idea that any government program is free or fully paid for demonstrates a complete lack of understanding of basic accounting and economics. Wake up, people, there is no such thing as a free lunch!

Governments have no money. They either take it from us, we the people, or they create it from thin air by printing more money. Balancing the budget or paying for government programs by printing more money doesn't end well. Just ask the people in Argentina or Venezuela.

The much ballyhooed Build Back Better spendathon program was hyped with the statement "And it is fully paid for and will reduce the deficit." Imagine that. Not only is it free but it also pays off some of the enormous government debt. That oceanfront swampland in Florida is sounding better every day. A Whitehouse Briefing Room statement dated October 28, 2021, notes that the proposed Build Back Better legislation is fully paid for only after significantly increasing taxes on corporations and on those evil millionaires and billionaires and after collecting untold sums from rich tax cheaters (no mention of collecting from poor tax cheaters). Fully paid for may make a great soundbite but it's basically a lie.

The lesson here is very simple. Governments, especially the Federal Government, need to develop balanced budgets on a regular basis, pass those budgets under regular government order rules and strictly abide by those budgets.

Voters need to find candidates who are capable and prepared to do just that. Then get them on the ballot and elect them.

LESSON TWELVE ☆ ☆ ☆
IMMIGRATION POLICY

U.S. immigration policy has been a political hot button for many years but the recent surges in illegal crossings at our southern border have raised this issue to new heights. We hear repeated claims of a broken immigration system. What does that mean? What exactly is broken?

We need to start with a common understanding of the term immigrant. The Migration Policy Institute, in a February 11, 2021, article[21] by Jeanne Batalova, Mary Hanna, and Christopher Levesque note that "foreign born" and "immigrant" are used interchangeably and refer to persons with no U.S. citizenship at birth. This population includes naturalized citizens, lawful permanent residents, refugees and asylees, persons on certain temporary visas, and unauthorized immigrants.

This same article notes there were 44.9 million immigrants in the U.S. in 2019, making up 13.7 percent of the total U.S. population. Of these, 23.2 million were naturalized U.S. citizens. The foreign-born share of the U.S. population was nearly 10 percent in 1850 when such records were first collected by the U.S. census. It varied between 13 percent and 15 percent over the next 60 years from 1860 through 1920. Changes in immigration laws, the Great Depression, and World War II resulted in decreasing percentages of immigrants to as low as 4.7 percent in 1970. Since then, a host of factors including changes in U.S. immigration law abolishing national-origin admission quotas in 1965, the Refugee Act of

1980 and significant shifts in economic and political relationships worldwide have brought us back to 15 percent, similar to levels we saw in the early twentieth century. Looking at immigration in this broader context, it seems relatively stable. So why all the fuss?

What is Immigration Policy and why do we need one? Bill Bennett, former secretary of education under Ronald Reagan, uses the "gate test" as a basis for determining the starting point for any immigration policy. Someone can judge a country by which direction people run when the country erects gates: Do they flee in, or do they risk life and limb to get out?

In the 1961, the East German Government built a wall to keep East Germans from escaping into West Germany. For the next 28 years, East Germans risked life and limb to get out. Many were killed trying to escape to the west. To my knowledge, there was no wall on the eastern borders of East Germany. Apparently escaping into Poland or Czechoslovakia wasn't all that enticing.

We have the opposite problem. People from all over the world are clamoring to get in to the U.S. We don't yet have walls, at least not completed walls, but we do we have lots of gates, better known as border crossing points. Many people aren't willing to get in line and follow the legal process to go through those gates. Instead, they avoid the gates by paying outrageous sums to criminals and cartels, risking life and limb to get into this country illegally.

There really is a U.S. immigration policy. It is a series of laws, regulations and directives put in place over many years to control and manage the flow of people into our country. It's a one-way policy. As far as I know, there aren't any restrictions against leaving the country unless there is a warrant for your arrest or you haven't paid your taxes in which case the IRS will track you down.

U.S. Immigration laws have been in place for more than 230 years, starting with the Nationality Act[22] of 1790. This was the first law to define eligibility for citizenship by naturalization and established standards and procedures by which immigrants could become U.S. citizens. Since then almost one hundred additional Congressional actions or Supreme Court decisions or Presidential orders have modified the process and left us with the so-called Immigration Policy we have today.

A sampling of changes made along the way include an 1849 Supreme Court decision confirming immigration issues were a federal responsibility, not subject to state or local authority, the 14th Amendment granting equal treatment for African-Americans after the Civil War, several laws and regulations dealing with Chinese immigrants during the later half of the nineteenth into the early twentieth centuries, and creation of the Immigration Bureau in 1891 which centralized immigration policy enforcement authority and processing responsibility within the federal government. The H-2 Guestworker Visa Program permitting temporary visas for farm workers was created in 1952. The Hart-Cellar Act of 1965 established the immigration quota policy still in place today (family reunification 75%, employment 20%, refugees 5%). The Department of Homeland Security (DHS) was created in 2002 by consolidating 22 diverse agencies and bureaus, putting responsibility for all immigration and border control issues under one overall agency. Time will judge the wisdom of that decision.

Where has this left us?

There are four basic immigration statuses: citizens, residents, nonimmigrants and undocumented immigrants.

In this case Citizens are foreign-born people who have been naturalized, becoming U.S. citizens under the auspices of the U.S. Citizenship and Immigration Services (USCIS) agency within the U.S. Department of Homeland Security. There were a total of 23.2 million[23] naturalized citizens in the U.S. in 2019.

Residents are lawful permanent residents (LPRs), more commonly known as green card holders, and 625,400 of them became U.S. citizens[24] during fiscal year 2020.

The nonimmigrant status group is a real challenge. From the Migration

Policy Institutes report noted earlier, 42.7 million people entered the U.S. under I-94 nonimmigrant status visas in 2016, the most recent year data was available from DHS. That's 42.7 million people in only one year.

Some of those entries were made on a short-term or an even daily basis such as attending business meetings, truck drivers delivering goods from across the border, airline crew members entering the U.S. and waiting for departure on their next flight, and visitors from Mexican or Canadian border towns coming for a day's shopping in the U.S. Others are longer-term entries including students, seasonal workers, and foreign military or government postings in the U.S. There are thirty-five types of temporary visas[25] spanning everything from type A for foreign government officials and diplomats, type B-2 for medical treatment or tourism, type H2-A for seasonal agricultural workers, type L for intra company transfers, all the way to types T-1 and U-1 covering human trafficking victims and victims of crime or criminal activity.

Is it any wonder dealing with immigration policy is such a nightmare?

The fourth immigration status is undocumented immigrants and is the source of most of the political fireworks surrounding immigration policy. MPI estimates around 11 million undocumented immigrants were living in the U.S. in 2019. There are other widely varying estimates, some more than double that amount depending on which news outlet or talking heads you use as your source of information. Not only is the total number of illegals in question, where they are located in the U.S. is often unknown.

U.S. immigration policy has been in place for almost as long as the U.S. has existed. That policy has evolved and adapted to accommodate the social and economic conditions of the time. For the most part, the immigration system seems to work fairly well. Think of the hundreds of thousands of people who enter our country legally every day under the various processes noted above. So why all the commotion about our broken immigration policy?

The Congressional Handbook

Some politicians, bureaucrats, and members of the general public aren't happy with parts of the policy. Some want more restrictive immigration policies, some want less restrictions and some seem to believe abolishing our national borders would be a sound choice. Balancing these incompatible ideals requires political wisdom and dexterity that is totally lacking in Congress today.

Politicians don't seem prepared to identify and make the necessary policy changes that could solve the supposed immigration problem. Instead, they selectively fail to enforce parts of the policy by underfunding border patrol operations, reducing deportations, and releasing apprehended illegal border crossers into the U.S. without any obvious penalty. If you are a foreign national who wants to get in to the U.S., why bother going through the narrow gate when you can just walk around it? Everyone sees the caravans marching in our direction yet the problem remains unresolved while the politicians continue using it as a talking point for the next election cycle.

Our immigration policy has evolved over many decades. Solving some of its serious shortcomings won't happen overnight. Achieving sustainable long-term solutions requires improving our basic understanding of our cultures, our traditions, and what it means to be an American. Teaching this to our children at the early elementary school level is a good place to start.

A full and balanced set of lessons is required including regular discussions of the pledge of allegiance. Rational classroom discussions, not required daily recitations since that was determined to be unconstitutional in a 1943 Supreme Court decision. Lessons about America as a melting pot of immigrants and citizens is critical. Learning about different viewpoints, cultures, and traditions and having respect for those differences in our society can be invigorating. Talk of identity politics and victimhood or transforming our society based on ill-advised theories or revisionist views of history are completely contrary to this concept.

America is the world's cocktail shaker, blending multiple cultures

D. M. Riach

(flavors) to gain strength for all by adopting the best from each and straining out the weak and irrational concepts (ice and pits). Responsible immigration policy is what has and will continue to keep this country the beacon it has always been. Our politicians and bureaucrats as well as the voting public all need a refresher course on this concept.

LESSON THIRTEEN ☆ ☆ ☆
EDUCATION

This lesson looks at two distinct parts of the multi-faceted education process in this country.

First is the education of our youth, from early childhood through to the young adult years. This is the aspect most people think about when they hear the term education.

Primary education is the responsibility of the parents, supported by their family and the community in which they live. Parents exercise this responsibility through locally elected schoolboards organized under the education regulations of each state. There is no role or need for federal government involvement anywhere in this process.

Teachers play a critical role in the education process, using their skills and experience to effectively pass knowledge and information on to the students in accordance with the parents' wishes. This crucial process must not be impeded by counterproductive ideologies or misguided aspirations of rogue schoolboards, teachers unions, or community organizers.

The education of our children is undoubtedly the most consequential action taken by parents during their lifetime. For some time, perhaps a couple generations, people didn't appreciate the significance of this responsibility. The Covid-19 pandemic and the reactions to it suddenly brought this dereliction of duty under the spotlight.

Lockdowns and school closures meant online learning was forced into homes where parents began to see what their children were being subjected to in the classrooms. They were not being taught how to think, how the basic functions of society really work, how to communicate (the first two of the three "Rs," reading, 'riting and 'rithmatic). Instead they were being indoctrinated with biased social ideals completely at odds with learning basic principles that would enable them to grow, prosper, and take care of themselves in the future. After a couple of generations of this kind of unbalanced teaching we are seeing the results in some recently elected members of Congress.

Fortunately we are starting to see positive changes at the local schoolboard level and even in gubernatorial elections.

Voter education is another critical but underappreciated and mostly forgotten aspect of our education system, a subject that desperately needs more attention as evidenced by the chaotic state of affairs we see in our federal and many of our state governments. Perhaps it is not so much a lack of education as it is an excess of misinformation, the current politically correct term for boldfaced lies.

Misinformation is rampant often on both sides of any particular issue. It is obvious to anyone with even the hint of a heartbeat that the main street media including the few remaining national or regional newspapers, old line TV networks and glaringly leftwing cable networks are all openly favoring the socialist, big government view of how the world should work. They endorse and actively promote candidates and policies of this bent.

Equally fervent but less numerous are the few newspapers and cable TV networks along with popular talk radio show hosts promoting conservative, small government and personal responsibility policies.

No doubt there are a range of opinions between these two distinct left/right visions. All of this is just fine, the strength of our free and open society is based on such diversity of opinion. What is missing is teaching the voter to recognize that these multiple viewpoints and biases exist and how to separate real truth from political truth (does Fake News really exist).

EPILOGUE

"When you see that in order to produce, you need to obtain permission from men who produce nothing—When you see that money is flowing to those who deal, not in goods, but in favors—When you see that men get richer by graft and by pull than by work, and your laws don't protect you against them, but protect them against you—When you see corruption being rewarded and honesty becoming a self-sacrifice—You may know that your society is doomed."

Ayn Rand
Atlas Shrugged, 1957

REFERENCES

1. https://www.govinfo.gov/content/pkg/GPO-CONAN-REV-2016/pdf/GPO-CONAN-REV-2016.pdf

2 https://www.heritage.org/election-integrity/heritage-explains/voter-fraud

3 https://www.fec.gov/about/mission-and-history/

4 https://ballotpedia.org/Federal_campaign_finance_laws_and_regulations#Bipartisan_Campaign_Reform_Act

5 https://home.howstuffworks.com/toilet2.htm

6 https://www.bridgemi.com/michigan-government/demystifying-michigan-elections-what-happens-ballots-after-you-vote

7 https://www.ncsl.org/research/elections-and-campaigns/primary-types.aspx

8 https://my.clevelandclinic.org/health/diseases/21590-bubonic-plague#

9 https://www.cdc.gov/flu/pandemic-resources/1918-pandemic-h1n1.html

10 https://www.census.gov/data/tables/time-series/demo/international-programs/historical-est-worldpop.html

11 Emergency Management Act, 1976 PA 390, as amended, MCL 30.403(4),

12 https://geology.utah.gov/map-pub/survey-notes/glad-you-asked/ice-ages-what-are-they-and-what-causes-them/

13 https://www.ncei.noaa.gov/news/day-historic-krakatau-eruption-1883

14 https://www.dni.gov/files/ODNI/documents/assessments/Prelimary-Assessment-UAP-20210625.pdf

15 https://www.npr.org/sections/thetwo-way/2013/08/16/212549163/there-it-is-area-51-revealed-in-declassified-cia-report

16 https://www.foia.gov/faq.html

17 https://www.justice.gov/sites/default/files/oip/legacy/2014/07/23/amendment-s2488.pdf

18 https://www.justice.gov/oip/blog/foia-post-2008-oip-guidance-segregating-and-marking-documents-release-accordance-open

19 https://www.chemicalsafetyfacts.org/dose-makes-poison-gallery/

20 Beyond Biden by Newt Gingrich – Pg. 120 11/18/2021

21 https://www.migrationpolicy.org/article/frequently-requested-statistics-immigrants-and-immigration-united-states

22 https://immigrationhistory.org/timeline/

23 https://www.migrationpolicy.org/article/naturalization-trends-united-states#

24 https://www.uscis.gov/citizenship-resource-center/naturalization-statistics

25 https://www.bankbazaar.com/visa/types-of-us-visa.html